Sicily
IN THE KITCHEN

30 recipes that are too good to miss!

MARIA TERESA DI MARCO - MARIE CÉCILE FERRÉ
PHOTOGRAPHY BY MAURIZIO MAURIZI

PICCOLI SPUNTINI

Guido Tommasi Editore
dal 1999

Summary

""To have seen Italy without having seen
Sicily is not to have seen Italy at all,
for Sicily is the clue to everything."
Goethe, *Italian Journey,*
13th April 1787

Sicilian cuisine is the cuisine of the *curtigghiu*, or the courtyard, with recipes being passed from door to door, from balcony to balcony and, literally, from mouth to mouth. Yet, at the same time, Sicilian cuisine is a cuisine which competes with the greatest of gastronomic traditions: the Arab tradition of sweet and sour, the French tradition of creative chefs, the farming tradition which skilfully uses the produce of the land. While there are a thousand variations each one is naturally the best, triggering endless arguments regarding authenticity of ingredients, cooking methods, the gallantry of suppliers, the proud boasts of a market. And so the task of describing and demonstrating a cuisine which is a world of flavours and ingredients proves to be not just difficult but, literally, "dangerous".
So as not to lose our bearings we clung to what seemed most familiar and sensible in order to sort out the muddle, interrogating grandmothers, aunts and friends from one coast to another on what is certainly an island but perhaps can best be described as a continent. This is why these are just some of the dishes which tell the story of Sicily, a small but significant description of Mediterranean tastes which are constantly changing. By word of mouth, from mouthful to mouthful, our book on Sicilian cuisine is not just a book written by three authors but the sum of many voices and, we would like to think, faces.

to Anna
who is on every page

ARANCINE DI RISO (Stuffed rice croquettes)

For approximately 25 arancine

- 1 kg of risotto rice (Arborio or Roma)
- 1 sachet or 6 threads of saffron
- 4 eggs
- 80 g of grated Pecorino cheese

For the classic filling:
- 500 g of mixed beef and pork
  (minced meat is fine if you are a hurry)
- 1 white onion
- 1 carrot
- 1 stick of celery
- 1 kg of ripe tomatoes (or 800 g of good quality
  tinned tomatoes, if out of season)

- 1 tablespoon of doubly concentrated tomato paste
  ('strattu)
- a few bay leaves
- 1 glass of full-bodied red wine
- extra virgin olive oil
- a few leaves of basil
- salt and pepper
- 180 g of Caciocavallo cheese
- 200 g of peas cooked with a little onion

For the breadcrumb coating:
- 3-4 eggs
- breadcrumbs (made from durum wheat bread) to
  taste

Boil the rice in a little lightly salted water until *al dente* and drain. Leave to rest for at least two hours or, better still, overnight.

Make the sauce by sautéing the onion, celery and carrot in a little extra virgin olive oil and then add the meat, tomato paste and wine. Once the wine has evaporated add the tomatoes with their skins and seeds removed, the bay leaves and the basil, salt, pepper and a glass of water. Lower the heat and continue to cook for about two hours mixing often and adding, if necessary, a few tablespoons of hot water, while taking care not to make the mixture too watery. When cooked chop the meat with a mezzaluna knife and keep the sauce to one side. Combine the rice with the Pecorino cheese, the beaten egg and the saffron dissolved in just a little warm water. In the palm of your hand pick up a fistful of rice and mould it into the shape of a small bowl. With the thumb of your other hand press down in the centre so as to form a hollow. Stuff with a tablespoon of the meat filling, add a small piece of Caciocavallo cheese and seal with more rice to form a ball or, following Catania tradition, an oval shape. While preparing the *arancini* you should rinse your hands often with very cold water. Once they are made dip them in the beaten egg, roll them in the breadcrumbs and fry them in plenty of piping hot oil for a few minutes. They should be served and eaten straightaway.

The name, like the shape, varies, as does everything else from the east to the west of the island. In Palermo they are called *arancine* and are round like oranges. In Catania they are called *arancini* and are tapered.

PASTA À LA NORMA

For 4 people

- 400 g of spaghetti
- 2 large pale purple aubergines
- 1 kg of ripe tomatoes (or 500 g of tomato preserve, best if homemade, if tomatoes are out of season)
- 1 clove of garlic
- a few leaves of basil (or better still two small bunches of curly leaved basil)
- 200 g of baked ricotta
- 4 tablespoons of extra virgin olive oil
- 1 tablespoon of sugar
- salt to taste
- peanut oil for frying
- coarse salt

Peel the aubergines in alternating stripes, that is leaving some of the peel on, and then cut the aubergine into vertical slices about half a centimetre thick. Layer the aubergine slices in a largish container, sprinkling coarse salt between each layer. Put an upside down plate on top and weigh it down (for instance with a pan full of water) and leave the aubergines to sweat for at least two hours.
Then rinse the aubergines thoroughly in order to eliminate the salt, dry them on a clean cloth and then fry them in piping hot oil until they are golden. Keep to one side. Parboil the tomatoes for two minutes at the most, then skin them, remove the seeds and brown them in a pan with 4 tablespoons of extra virgin olive oil and a clove of garlic. Cook over a low heat until they are soft, then sieve them. Put the sauce back on the heat and allow it to thicken. Then add the basil, sugar and salt.
Cook the spaghetti until it is *al dente*, drain and dress with the tomato sauce and fried aubergine, sprinkle with the coarsely grated baked ricotta and add a few leaves of basil if you like.

PASTA WITH BREADCRUMBS

For 4 people

- 400 g of spaghetti (o bucatini pasta)
- 4 cloves of garlic (ideally from Nubia)
- 4 salted anchovy fillets
- 200 g of breadcrumbs (made from durum wheat flour bread)
- 5 tablespoons of extra virgin olive oil
- salt

Sauté the oil with the garlic in a large pan, add the thoroughly cleaned and rinsed anchovies and allow them to disintegrate. Turn off the heat and keep to one side.
In a second large pan toast the breadcrumbs over a lively heat stirring continuously with a wooden spoon as breadcrumbs tend to burn straightaway. As soon as they are a nice, toasty shade of brown, turn off the heat and take them out of the pan.
Cook the spaghetti until it is *al dente* in salted boiling water, fold it into the anchovy oil and serve with a generous sprinkling of toasted breadcrumbs.

If you are not afraid to use too much oil you can add another tablespoon to the toasting breadcrumbs, which will make them moister.

PESTO TRAPANI STYLE

For 4 people

- 400 g of spaghetti (or mafaldine pasta)
- 4 cloves of garlic (ideally from Nubia)
- 4 not too large ripe tomatoes
- 1 bunch of basil
- 3 tablespoons of almonds
- extra virgin olive oil
- coarse salt

Pound the garlic and basil with half a tablespoon of coarse salt in a wooden mortar until you obtain a creamy paste. Add the almonds and continue patiently to pound and amalgamate, drizzling the oil so that the end result is nice and smooth. Add the tomatoes with their skin and seeds removed and amalgamate them with the pesto. Add salt and a little more oil and then dress the pasta with the sauce.

SPAGHETTI WITH BOTARGO

For 4 people

- 400 g of spaghetti
- 4 tablespoons of grated botargo
- 1 clove of garlic
- 1 tablespoon of finely chopped parsley
- 8 tablespoons of extra virgin olive oil
- coarse salt

In a large pan sizzle the oil with the garlic for one minute, then turn off the heat and keep to one side. Cook the spaghetti until it is *al dente*. Drain but keep half a glass of the water. Put the spaghetti in the pan with the oil, add the grated botargo and toss over a lively heat adding a little of the water the spaghetti was cooked in if necessary. To serve, remove the garlic and sprinkle with the finely chopped parsley.

PASTA WITH SARDINES

For 4 people

- 400 g of bucatini pasta
- 400 g of sardines
- 1 bunch of wild fennel (about half a kilo uncooked)
- 50 g of sun-dried raisins
- 50 g of pine nuts
- 3 salted anchovies
- 1 sachet of saffron (better still a few threads)
- 1 onion
- extra virgin olive oil
- breadcrumbs

Clean the sardines, remove their heads, gut them and bone them. Rinse carefully and keep to one side. Parboil the fennel in plenty of salted water (which is the same water you will use for boiling the pasta) then drain it thoroughly with a perforated spoon and keep the water.

Chop the onion and sauté it with a few tablespoons of extra virgin olive oil. As soon as the onion is soft add the anchovies, rinsed of their salt and gutted, and then the raisins which have been previously been left to plump up in warm water, the pine nuts and the coarsely chopped wild fennel. Dilute the saffron in a glass of the water the fennel was cooked in, add it to the other ingredients and then add the sardines and wild fennel and proceed to cook in a covered pan.

In the meantime boil the pasta (in the water the fennel was cooked in), drain it and add it to the dressing, blending well.

Serve with a sprinkling of a tablespoon of toasted breadcrumbs as though it were grated cheese.

VARIANTS

Throughout Sicily the number of variants of this traditional dish is, as usual, and perhaps even more than usual, infinite.

There are those who make a red version with tomato paste, those who bake the dressed pasta in the oven, those who fry the sardines separately, those who use tons of toasted breadcrumbs and those who wouldn't even dream of using them, not to mention the variables in the quantities of ingredients. The only thing that doesn't change is the absolute freshness of the ingredients and the wonderful combination of raisins, saffron and wild fennel.

MACARONI TIMBALE

For 6/8 people

For the shortcrust pastry:
- 300 g of flour
- 125 g of butter
- 125 g of sugar
- 1 egg + 2 yolks
- 1 small glass of sweet wine (Marsala)
- 1 pinch of salt
- 1 egg for glazing

For the filling:
- 600 g of large macaroni
- 200 g of tomato sauce

- 300 g of béchamel
- 200 g of peas cooked with a little onion
- 300 g of chicken liver and giblets
- 100 g of dried mushrooms
- 150 g of Caciocavallo cheese
- 150 g of ham cut into strips
- 100 g of sausage
- 1 tablespoon of butter
- 1 small glass of sweet wine (Marsala)
- 2 bay leaves
- salt and pepper

Make the shortcrust pastry without kneading it for too long and keep it covered in the fridge.
Make the béchamel and the tomato sauce and keep both to one side.
Brown the liver with the bay leaves in a little butter, add the mushrooms softened in warm water, and leave to cook for a few minutes adding a splash of Marsala.
In a very large salad bowl mix the sausage, ham, Caciocavallo and peas and, once cooled, add the liver sauce.
Roll out three quarters of the shortcrust pastry into a disc measuring approximately 25 centimetres in diameter, with a thickness of approximately one centimetre, and use it to line a pie dish (preferably spring-form) all the way up to the rim.
Cook the macaroni and, when it is *al dente*, drain it, pour it into the salad bowl, add the tomato sauce and béchamel and mix thoroughly. Pour the mixture into the pie dish lined with the shortcrust pastry pressing it down lightly with the back of a spoon. Cover with a second disc of shortcrust pastry and seal the edges. Decorate it as you like, brush with the beaten egg and bake in a preheated oven at 180°C for about an hour.

Sicilian timbales are sumptuous and baroque by definition. There are aristocratic versions which require many other ingredients and many other steps, but this version, despite being modest, seems to us to be relatively easy both to make and to digest.

ILDAZZA'S PALERMITAN TIMBALE

For 8/10 people

- 1 kg of anellini pasta
- 1 kg of braising beef
- 1 bottle of tomato sauce
- 1 tablespoon of tomato extract (sometimes you can add a tablespoon more, it depends on the consistency of the sauce)
- 3 slices (just a little thicker than a finger) of fresh Caciocavallo cheese cut into cubes
- a quarter of a ripened Caciocavallo cheese grated

- peanut oil for frying
- 9-10 (thin) slices of mortadella sausage
- 12-15 thin slices of salami (the one with black peppercorns)
- 6-8 long aubergines sliced into the thickness of a finger
- salt, black pepper, extra virgin olive oil, breadcrumbs
- onion, garlic, a few bay leaves

Sauté the onion, garlic and a few bay leaves in 3 tablespoons of extra virgin olive oil and then brown the meat turning it on all sides. Add the tomato sauce and extract and leave it to cook slowly for at least two hours.

In the meantime prepare the aubergines.

Peel them and cut them lengthwise into slices that are approximately 1 cm thick and layer them, covered with a few handfuls of salt, in a colander under a weight, so that their bitter juices run. Wash them, dry them thoroughly and fry them in piping hot peanut oil. Pat them to remove the excess oil and keep to one side.

Once the meat is cooked chop it with a mezzaluna knife into small even-sized pieces and put back over the heat for about ten minutes together with the sauce, adding a little water if necessary.

Prepare the, preferably spring-form, tin by greasing it carefully and sprinkling it with breadcrumbs, then line it with the fried aubergines making sure they adhere to the bottom and sides.

Boil the anellini until it is *al dente*, stir it into the sauce and then spread a layer of the pasta on top of the layer of aubergines lining the bottom of the tin, followed by alternating layers of cheese, mortadella sausage and salami, all sprinkled with the grated Caciocavallo. Cover with a final layer of pasta and seal with the aubergines.

Bake in a preheated oven at 200°C for 20-30 minutes. Leave to cool, then turn out and serve.

The recipe for this Palermitan triumph comes to us, with Micaela as the go-between, from Ilde (affectionately nicknamed Ildazza, because she is the world's kindest and most patient person), who makes it with rigorous western precision, keen to underline that, in Palermo, eggs, boiled or beaten, are a heresy in a timbale. It is something that is only ever seen on the opposite side of the island, on the east coast....

COURGETTE SOUP

For 4 people

- 1 long, narrow courgette
- 3 ripe tomatoes
- 4 small potatoes
- 2 onions
- 100 g of peppery Pecorino cheese
- 4 tablespoons of extra virgin olive oil
- salt and pepper

Thinly slice the onions and brown them in the extra virgin olive oil, add the previously parboiled tomatoes, skinned and deseeded with a fork, and then the potato chopped into small chunks. Brown for a few minutes and then add the peeled courgette chopped into small pieces.
Add a glass of water (and a vegetable stock cube if necessary) and leave to cook over a low heat for 30-40 minutes. Then add the Pecorino cheese chopped into not too small pieces and the salt and pepper and reduce to your liking.

The soup is served hot or cold, depending on taste and climate.

MACCO VERDE DI FAVE (Green bean mush)

For 4 people

- about 500 g of shelled fresh broad beans.
  (calculate about 2 kg of broad beans in their pods)
- 3 spring onions
- 1 large bunch of wild fennel
- 4 tablespoons of extra virgin olive oil
- salt

Wash the wild fennel keeping the most tender tops to one side and parboiling the rest in salted boiling water. Drain but keep the broth.
Brown the chopped spring onions in extra virgin olive oil, add the broad beans and the wild fennel and cover the broad beans with a brimming cup of the water the fennel was boiled in. Cook until the broad beans are soft and begin to disintegrate, then "dent them" with a spoon or, in other words, make them mushy. Serve with a drizzle of extra virgin olive oil and the tops of the wild fennel.

There are infinite versions of the *macco*. The most popular recipe calls for dried broad beans instead of fresh ones as they can be found all year round but this greener version has a unique flavour. Often broken bits of pasta are added to the mush and, if there is any dried broad bean *macco* leftover the next day, it can be made into fritters.

MEAT ON LEMON LEAVES

For 4 people

- about twenty medium-sized lemon leaves
- 600 g of very lean minced beef (such as tartare)
- a little fresh tomato
- 1 clove of garlic
- the grated rind of one lemon
- 5 tablespoons of extra virgin olive oil
- salt

Wash the lemon leaves thoroughly, first soaking them in cold water and then rubbing them under running water, and dry well. Use your hands to mix the skinned and deseeded tomato chopped into small pieces, the minced garlic, the grated lemon peel, the salt and the olive oil with the minced meat.
In the palm of your hand form elongated and flattened meat patties and place each one on a lemon leaf. Cover with a second leaf. Cook briefly in the oven (under the grill) or, if you are lucky enough to have one, use a barbecue.

It is worth the bother to track down lemon leaves (but make sure they are healthy and haven't been treated with chemicals!) in order to try cooking meat using this method. It is almost unbelievable how much fragrance a lemon leaf contains and you will see, at least in this case, how tempted you will be to eat the leaf!

AUNT GRAZIELLA'S MESSINA STYLE ROULADES

For 4 people

- 400 g of thin slices of pork loin or, alternatively, veal rump
- 150 g of soft Sicilian Pecorino cheese (or, in the absence of this, Provolone Dolce)
- 1 white onion or 2 tender spring onions
- 200 g of breadcrumbs
- 50 g of grated Parmesan or Pecorino cheese
- melted butter
- bay leaves
- salt and pepper

Wrap the slices of meat around a small piece of cheese and two or three small wedges of onion (the roulade must be no longer than a finger, about 7 cm). Thread the roulades onto skewers, alternating them with bay leaves and a few onion wedges if you like. Roll the skewers in the melted butter and then in the breadcrumbs mixed with the Parmesan. Season with salt and pepper and brown quickly on a barbecue or under an oven grill.

FALSO MAGRO

The name of the dish ("deceptively lean") says it all ...

For 6-8 people

- 1 approximately 600 g slice of beef
  (well beaten by the butcher)
- 150 g of minced beef
- 2 tablespoons of grated Pecorino cheese
- 4 tablespoons of breadcrumbs

For the stuffing:
- 4 boiled eggs
- 200 g slice of mortadella sausage
- 200 g of Caciocavallo cheese
- 100 g of thick slices of lard
- 2 tablespoons of extra virgin olive oil

For the sauce:
- 2 onions
- 2 carrots
- 1 stick of celery
- 400 g of tomato purée
- half a glass of full-bodied red wine
- 1 tablespoon of sugar
- 2 tablespoons of extra virgin olive oil

Lay the slice of beef on a work surface and spread it with a mixture of the minced beef, breadcrumbs and Pecorino cheese, leaving a space of two fingers along the edges. Lay the ingredients in regular alternating rows: a row of Mortadella cut into small, approximately 1 cm thick, strips, then a row of Caciocavallo cheese, then the eggs (again cut into strips), the lard and so on. Once you have used all the stuffing roll up the *falso magro* and tie it tightly with string so that the filling doesn't spill out.
Pour two tablespoons of oil into a large pan and sauté the *falso magro*, turning it to "seal" the meat. Then take it out of the pan and keep it to one side. Pour half a glass of water into the same pan and brown the finely chopped onions. When the water has evaporated add two tablespoons of oil, the chopped carrots and celery and the *falso magro*. Add the tomato and red wine mixed with the sugar and turn up the heat for a few minutes until the wine has evaporated. Add a glass of water, lower the heat as far as it will go and cook covered, stirring from time to time, for about 40 minutes. Turn off the heat and let it rest for a few hours in the pan. Overnight is best since the following day the *falso magro* will be even tastier.
Before serving remove the string (obviously!) and give yourself a round of applause!

STUFFED SARDINE ROLLS

For 4 people

- 500 g of sardines (not too big but not too small either)
- approximately 100 g of breadcrumbs
- 2 tablespoons of pine nuts
- 2 tablespoons of raisins
- 1 clove of garlic
- juice of one lemon
- extra virgin olive oil
- salt and pepper
- bay leaves

Patiently clean the sardines removing the bones and the head. Splay open and keep to one side. Toast the breadcrumbs in a thick-bottomed pan, stirring carefully with a wooden spoon until they are golden brown or, as they say in Sicily, "the shade of a monk's habit", then take them out of the pan (otherwise they will continue to toast) and, little by little, stir in the oil, the minced garlic, the pine nuts and the raisins plumped up in warm water.

When the mixture is thoroughly blended place a teaspoon of it on (the inside of) each sardine and roll the sardines up. Lay the sardine rolls in a tin greased with oil alternating them with the bay leaves and squeezing them in tightly so they won't open up during cooking. Squeeze the lemon juice and add salt, pepper and extra virgin olive oil to make a marinade to drizzle over the sardines, then bake them in a not too hot oven for about 10-15 minutes. They are also an absolute treat eaten cold.

STOCKFISH MESSINA STYLE

For 6 people

- 600 g of dried cod (stockfish) that has been soaked
- 400 g of potatoes
- 300 g of tomato purée
- 1 stick of celery
- 2 tablespoons of green olives
- 1 tablespoon of salted capers
- 1 tablespoon of pine nuts
- 1 tablespoon of raisins
- extra virgin olive oil
- salt and pepper

Quickly parboil the celery, including the greenest leaves chopped into small chunks, and keep to one side. Cook the tomato with a little extra virgin olive oil and add the potatoes chopped into medium-small pieces, the celery, the (thoroughly rinsed) capers, the olives, the pine nuts and the raisins. Pour enough water on top to cover the mixture and cook it for 10-15 minutes. Add the stockfish chopped into pieces and a little more water if required and cook for about half an hour over a gentle heat taking care not to break up the fish and the potatoes too much when stirring them. Add salt and pepper and serve hot or warm, although it's also delicious eaten cold.

TUNAFISH AND ONIONS

For 4 people

- 1 kg of extremely fresh tuna fish cut into approximately 1 cm thick slices
- 4 golden onions
- half a glass of vinegar
- 1 tablespoon of sugar
- 5 tablespoons of extra virgin olive oil
- mint to taste
- salt

Heat 3 tablespoons of oil in a large pan and quickly fry the slices of tuna fish, taking care not to dry them out. Sprinkle with a little salt.

Remove from the heat and arrange in an ovenproof dish.

Pour the remaining oil into the same pan and brown the onions sliced into not too thin rings until they are soft. Add the vinegar and the sugar and cook for a few minutes.

Pour the still hot onion sauce over the tuna fish, add the leaves of mint and patiently wait until it is cold before you eat it. It will be even tastier the following day.

SARDINE AND RAISIN RISSOLES

For 4 people

- 500 g of fresh sardines
- approximately 200 g of breadcrumbs
- 50 g of Pecorino cheese
- 2 eggs
- a handful of raisins
- half a fistful of pine nuts
- salt
- peanut oil for frying

Clean the sardines (this is the most time-consuming part), removing their heads, bones and tails and then wash them thoroughly, chop them with a broad-bladed knife and keep to one side.
Beat the eggs with a pinch of salt, add the breadcrumbs, the cheese, the raisins and the pine nuts, and, finally, the fish.
Form little patties with wet hands and fry them in plenty of piping hot oil.
Pat them with kitchen towel to eliminate the excess oil, sprinkle with salt and serve hot.

GLUTTONOUS SWORDFISH

For 4 people

- 1 kg of sliced swordfish
- 3 tinned tomatoes
- 1 onion
- 2 sticks of celery
- 150 g of green olives
- 40 g of capers
- 4 tablespoons of extra virgin olive oil

Parboil the celery (including the leaves) in a little lightly salted water, chop into small chunks and keep to one side.
Carefully rinse the salt from the capers, stone the olives and keep these to one side too.
Finely chop the onion and sauté it in a low-sided thick-bottomed pan with the extra virgin olive oil. When it is soft and golden add the celery, the olive and the capers, cook for a few more minutes and then add the tomatoes mashed with a fork and the sliced fish.
Leave to cook covered over a low heat for 15 minutes adding a little warm water if necessary.

ANCHOVIES WITH MINT

For 4 people

- 600 g of anchovies
- 2 juicy lemons
- 1 good-sized bunch of mint
- 3 cloves of garlic
- 5 tablespoons of extra virgin olive oil
- 2 teaspoons of sugar
- salt and pepper

Clean the anchovies, removing the heads, bones and tails, wash carefully and dry on a cloth. Grease the bottom of a low-sided pan with a tablespoon of oil and spread a layer of mint leaves and minced garlic on it, followed by a layer of anchovies. Pour a tablespoon of oil on top, add salt and pepper and then start again with the mint and garlic. Continue to do this until you have used up all the anchovies. Squeeze the two lemons and dissolve the sugar in the juice. Pour this over the layers of anchovies and cook covered over a gentle heat for about 30 minutes, "shaking" the pan from time to time but not stirring with a fork.

The anchovies or, as they are known on the east coast, the *masculini*, will taste delicious after they have been left to rest for a few hours.

ENZA'S COUSCOUS

For the semolina:
- 1 kg of couscous semolina (coarse grained durum wheat)
- water, oil, salt, pepper, garlic

For the fish "broth":
- 1 kg of assorted fish for soup, preferably a variety of very small fish, but also prawns and seafood
- 300-400 g of ripe tomatoes (or good quality tinned tomatoes if tomatoes are out of season)
- 1 onion
- 2 cloves of garlic

For the fish soup:
- 800 g of assorted fish for soup including, if you can find it, scorpionfish but also mussels, prawns, clams
- 300 g of ripe tomatoes (or good quality tinned tomatoes if tomatoes are out of season)
- 1 onion
- 1 clove of garlic
- 6 tablespoons of extra virgin olive oil
- 1 chilli pepper

For the pesto:
- 3 cloves of garlic (ideally from Nubia)
- 4-5 almonds
- 1 small bunch of parsley

Make a fish soup by sautéing the onion with the garlic and chilli pepper in the oil, adding the tomatoes and the fish and covering everything with plenty of water (approximately 2 litres). Leave to cook slowly until the fish has disintegrated. Then put everything through a food mill and keep the stock.

Make a pesto by pounding the garlic with the parsley and the almonds in a mortar. As soon as it is ready add it to the soup and cover immediately with a lid to trap the fragrance.

Follow the same procedure for the second batch of fish soup, the one with the large fish and the mussels. Avoid sieving by simply reducing the quantity of water.

Make the semolina. Be warned! This is the trickiest bit!

Place a *mafararda* (a large conical terracotta dish which is used expressly for this purpose) on the table. Place the salted water and the semolina to the left of the *mafararda*. Place a little semolina, approximately three fistfuls, in the bottom of the *mafararda* and, using your left hand, spoon in some water so that it runs down the side of the *mafararda* while you simultaneously moisten the semolina by rotating it in your right hand. This operation is known as *incocciata*. Take it slowly: the dry semolina must be moistened while you add it a little at a time to the bowl. Enza first moistens the semolina a little more than is strictly necessary only to achieve the correct degree of moistness by continuing to add dry semolina to the bowl.

When the couscous is ready it must be turned out onto a clean cloth and spread out with your hands to dry. It is best to make the semolina the night before so that it is very dry but, in any case, it must be left to dry for at least one and a half hours.

Take the cloth by the edges and pour the entire contents into the *mafararda*, dress with plenty of oil, salt, pepper and the garlic which has been pounded and reduced to a cream and amalgamate everything by rolling the balls of semolina between the palms of your hands to impregnate them well, lifting the couscous from the bottom of the bowl.

Take a *couscoussier* (a special pan also made of perforated terracotta like a colander) and put plenty of coarsely chopped onion and the bay leaves in the bottom. Pour the couscous on top and balance the *couscoussier* on top of another high-sided pan (like a saucepan for cooking pasta) full of cold water, taking care that the bottom of the *couscoussier* does not touch the water.

Make a very sticky dough of flour and water which will be used to "glue" the *couscoussier* dish to the top of the pan underneath to stop the steam dissipating while it is cooking. Use your fingers to make a rope to seal the two pans, then place over the heat and put a lid on the *couscoussier*. Enza advises setting the heat to high and waiting for the steam to rise from the couscous. As soon as the steam appears we say that the couscous has been "dispatched" and from that moment on you should calculate 1 hour and 15 minutes to cook it. Keep the lid partially raised by inserting a spoon so that the steam condensation doesn't make the semolina too damp and lower the heat so as not to risk losing all the water. If that were to happen the couscous would taste burnt and be inedible.

The couscous must be stirred from time to time while it is being cooked, always applying the same technique, beginning at the bottom and moving to the top.

Once it is cooked slit the pastry rope with a knife, lift the *couscoussier* and pour the couscous into the *mafararda*.

At this point the couscous must be generously "watered" with the previously made fish broth to make it nice and moist. Then it must be covered with a clean cloth and wrapped in a blanket.

Leave it to rest in the blanket for at least half an hour to give it time to swell up.

Serve it (proudly!) with the leftover broth, so that it can be moistened some more, and with the soup made of large fish.

The quantities of couscous are based not so much on the number of people to feed but on the capacity of the special pan it is cooked in. The one we used, a gift from Enza, contained a kilo of semolina and fed 6 (but maybe even 8) people comfortably.

On this occasion we did things in style and made a double batch of fish soup: the first, which was sieved, was used to moisten the semolina, while the point of the second, made with whole pieces of fish, was to give the diners the pleasant sensation of biting into the flesh of the fish. But even with just one batch of soup the recipe works beautifully, as well as being quite labour-intensive enough....

Enza is from Trapani and is a force to be reckoned with: four children, a demanding job, a kitchen blog (iodagrande.blogspot.com) and bags of surplus energy. She gave us the gift of her couscous which is an absolute concentration of experience and alchemy, so fragrant it is worth making the effort to try and learn it from her.

GRANDMA PINA'S AUBERGINE PARMIGIANA

For 10/12 people

- 3 round purple aubergines
- 5 hard-boiled eggs
- 400 g of tomato sauce
- 250 g of Provola Dolce cheese
- 4 tablespoons of Parmesan
- 3 tablespoons of breadcrumbs
- peanut oil for frying
- 1 clove of garlic
- a few leaves of basil

Peel the aubergines lengthwise and slice them, then place them in layers in a colander and cover each layer with a handful of coarse salt. Cover with an upside down plate and something to weigh it down. The aubergines will sweat out their bitter juices and won't be so oily when fried.

After about one hour rinse the aubergines and dry them carefully with a clean cloth, then fry and keep to one side.

Make a tomato sauce flavoured with a clove of garlic and a few leaves of fresh basil. Cook the eggs and slice them thinly.

Lightly grease an ovenproof dish or pan and sprinkle with the breadcrumbs, eliminating any surplus.

Place a layer of fried aubergines, then a layer of egg and one of cheese, cover with a few tablespoons of tomato sauce and two tablespoons of grated Parmesan. Then place another layer of aubergine, one of egg, one of cheese, the sauce and the Parmesan.

Finish off with a final layer of fried aubergine, a few more tablespoons of sauce and a mixture of breadcrumbs and Parmesan. Place in a previously heated piping hot oven, but immediately lower the temperature to 160°C and cook for about 30 minutes until a crispy golden crust has formed.

Once out of the oven the *parmigiana* must be left to rest for at least a couple of hours but if you can manage to wait until the following day it will be even tastier.

Aubergine *parmigiana* is one of Sicily's most experimented dishes. Every *parmigiana* is an individual work, the result of different ingredients, cooking times and oven settings. It goes without saying that everyone thinks their *parmigiana* is the best and we are no exception to the rule, if only to honour the tradition.

PEPPERS IN RED WINE

For 4 people

- 5 large meaty peppers of various colours
- 2 crushed cloves of garlic
- half a glass of *vino cotto*
- extra virgin olive oil
- salt and pepper

Cut the peppers into thick strips after removing the seeds and the stalk. Wash them and place them still damp in a pan in a preheated oven with half a glass of water. Turn them every so often.
When they are soft transfer the pan to the top of the stove, brown in oil, add two crushed cloves of garlic, salt and pepper and, finally, a few tablespoons of *vino cotto*.

If you cannot find *vino cotto* you can substitute it with a full-bodied red wine, reduced with a little sugar. It won't be the same but it will render the idea.

CAPONATA DI MELANZANE DI ANNA
(Anna's aubergine stew)

For 6 people

- 6 round aubergines with a pale purple skin
- 4 cloves of garlic
- the hearts of two stalks of green celery
- 4 skinned ripe tomatoes
- 200 g of green olives
- 3 tablespoons of salted capers
- 100 g of pine nuts
- 150 g of raisins
- half a glass of red wine vinegar
- 2 tablespoons of sugar
- a few leaves of basil
- oil
- salt and pepper

Chop the aubergine into cubes and put them in a large colander. Sprinkle with coarse salt and leave under a weight for at least two hours so that all their bitter juices run out. Then rinse them, dry them and fry them in boiling oil. Keep to one side.

Pour the used oil into a large pan with low sides and sauté the cloves of garlic, the celery (stalks and leaves shredded and blanched), the chopped skinned tomatoes with their seeds removed, the olives which have been stoned and cut into quarters, the capers rinsed of salt, the pine nuts and the raisins. Cook until the celery is soft and then add the aubergine with a few leaves of basil.

Continue to cook for another ten minutes over a low heat, stirring frequently. Then sprinkle the *caponata* with the sugar dissolved in the vinegar.

Mix well and add salt and pepper. Serve cold after it has rested for a few hours.

The recipe for this *caponata* is special because it is Anna's. We miss her terribly. Her *caponata* was always perfect.

ROAST ARTICHOKES

For 4 people

- 4 artichokes (the purple ones if possible)
- 2 cloves of garlic
- 6 tablespoons of breadcrumbs
- 4 tablespoons of grated Caciocavallo cheese (or peppery Pecorino)
- 1 small bunch of parsley
- extra virgin olive oil
- salt

Clean the artichokes by scraping the stalks and eliminating the outer leaves only.
Mince the garlic with the parsley, add the breadcrumbs and the grated cheese and mix well.
Bang the artichokes on the table so that the leaves open slightly, then stuff the space between the leaves with the garlic mixture, pressing it down with your fingers to the base of the artichoke. Lightly salt each artichoke and moisten with a trickle of extra virgin olive oil, then grill until they are thoroughly toasted on all sides.

Charcoal is ideal for grilling artichokes. They should be three quarters buried in the ash where they will cook uniformly and develop a unique flavour. In the absence of charcoal a barbecue or even an oven grill will do just fine.

SQUASH WITH BLACK OLIVES

For 4 people

- 800 g of yellow squash
- 20-25 black olives
- 2 tablespoons of vinegar
- 2 tablespoons of extra virgin olive oil
- 1 tablespoon of sugar
- peanut oil for frying
- salt

Peel the squash and cut it into small slices about half a centimetre thick, then fry it in plenty of peanut oil and dry it on kitchen towel.
Remove the oil from the pan but don't wash it. Pour in the vinegar in which you have dissolved the sugar, then the extra virgin olive oil, the olives and half a tablespoon of salt. As soon as the mixture begins to sizzle, remove it from the heat and use it to dress the fried squash.

FROZEN LEMON

For 6 people

- 80 g of wheat starch
- 250 g of sugar
- 1 l of water
- the grated peel and juice of 3 lemons (fresh, organic and possibly green)

Wash the lemons, dry them and grate the peel, taking care not to damage the pith (which would give the gelo a bitter taste). Leave the grated peel to infuse in water overnight. Filter the water with the grated peel, add the sieved wheat starch, diluting it first in a little of the juice, and then add the sugar, taking care not to form lumps.
Bring to the boil and then add the filtered juice of the three lemons and cook for another one or two minutes.
Pour into a mould and leave to cool (in the fridge) for at least 3-4 hours.

CANNOLI

This recipe is a gift from Gianna, who came to Sicilian cuisine by way of love. The love of a Sicilian obviously.

For 10 cannoli

For the casings:
- 300 g of flour
- 30 g of sugar
- 25 g of butter
- 15 g of unsweetened cocoa powder (we added this bit)
- 1 small glass of dry Marsala
- 1 pinch of salt
- 1 egg white

For the filling:
- 300 g of sheep's ricotta
- 150 g of icing sugar
- 50 g candied orange peel
- 50 g of dark chocolate chips
- one small glass of rum (optional)
- peanut oil or lard for frying

Sieve the flour and add the sugar, the salt and the cocoa powder and then the butter and the Marsala. Knead until you have an elastic and very soft amber-coloured pastry. Roll into a ball, wrap in cling film and leave to rest in the fridge for about an hour. In the meantime make the filling. Finely sieve the ricotta and add the sugar, then beat the mixture until it is very puffy and glossy. Add the candied peel and the chocolate chips and, if you like, flavour it with the liqueur. Keep the cream covered in the fridge so that it does not absorb any odours.
Retrieve the dough and roll it out with a rolling pin until it is a few millimetres thick. Cut out oval shapes and wrap them around cannoli moulds (nowadays made of steel but traditionally made of bamboo cane) and seal the edges in the centre with a little egg white. Heat the oil (or, better still, the lard) in a high-sided pan and, when it is just beginning to smoke, immerse the whole cannoli. Cook them for a few short minutes and then remove them with a perforated spoon and leave them to drain on kitchen towel. Once they are cold extract them from the moulds. Only fill the cannoli when you are ready to eat them, otherwise the casing will turn soggy.

CASSATA

Cassata is a sweet you can make at home. It just requires a little patience and manual skill in order to assemble and decorate it. The reward is the sweetest of satisfactions.

For the sponge:
- 5 eggs
- 140 g of sugar
- 140 g of flour and potato starch in equal parts
- 1 pinch of salt

For the filling:
- 700 g of extremely fresh sheep's ricotta
- 180 g of icing sugar
- 70 g of dark chocolate chips
- 80 g of small pieces of candied peel

For the pastry:
- a 250 g stick of almond paste
- green food colouring

For the icing:
- 1 egg white
- 175 g of icing sugar
- 1 tablespoon of lemon juice

More:
- Marsala (or a different liqueur) to moisten the sponge
- candied peel to decorate

The evening before sieve the ricotta , add the sugar and beat until extremely creamy. Keep the mixture in the fridge in a bowl covered with cling film. Make the sponge. Beat the egg yolks with the sugar in a large bowl until you have obtained a very pale and frothy mixture. Combine the salt, the sieved flour and potato starch and add to the dough kneading for about ten minutes. Beat the egg whites separately and, when they are stiff, add them too, stirring from bottom to top so as to avoid creating air bubbles. Pour into a well-greased (preferably spring-form) mould and bake in a preheated oven for about 40 minutes at 180°C. Once cold cut into slices to line the cassata on the top and on the bottom.
Knead the almond paste on a work surface sprinkled with icing sugar, add the food colouring until you get a shade of green you like and then roll it out with a rolling pin and cut a strip of the same thickness as the side of the dish you are using.
Line a conical dish about 30 cm in diameter with cling film. Place the strip of green coloured almond paste around the edge and a layer of sponge on the bottom. Moisten with plenty of Marsala (or another sweet liqueur) mixed with water, then cover with the ricotta cream, to which you have added the candied peel and chocolate. Cover with more slices of sponge, which you will moisten with liqueur. Place an upside down plate on top of the cassata and keep it in the fridge for a few hours.
Make the icing by beating the egg white with the sugar until stiff and adding the lemon little by little. Having decided to decorate only the top of the sweet with icing we have kept the icing quite stiff. If you want it to run down the edges add a little lemon juice and slightly reduce the quantity of sugar.
Turn the cassata out into a serving dish, pour the icing on the top of the sweet and spread it so that it is even. Decorate with the candied peel and, just for fun, draw a pattern on the green edge with the leftover icing.

MINNE DI SANT'AGATA (Saint Agatha's bosoms)

For 20-24 minne

For the shortcrust pastry:
- 300 g of flour
- 125 g of butter
- 125 g of sugar
- 1 egg+ 2 yolks
- 1 pinch of salt
- vanilla flavouring (or better still, vanilla pod seeds)

For the icing:
- 350 g of icing sugar
- 2 tablespoons of lemon juice
- 2 egg whites
- glacé cherries to decorate

For the filling:
- 600 g of sheep's ricotta
- 80 g of small pieces of candied peel
- 100 g of dark chocolate flakes
- 100 g of icing sugar

Make the shortcrust pastry by mixing the chopped butter with the flour, the sugar, a pinch of salt and vanilla and by blending in the eggs one by one. Once you have a smooth dough make a ball, cover and keep in the fridge.
Make the filling. Sieve the ricotta and beat it with the icing sugar until you have a very soft and frothy cream. Add the candied peel and the chocolate flakes and leave to rest in the fridge for about an hour. Roll out the shortcrust pastry into a rather thin sheet (about half a centimetre thick) and use it to line lightly greased round moulds. Fill with the ricotta mixture and cover with a smaller disk of shortcrust pastry (if you haven't got a round mould you can use a champagne goblet to make the round shape of the minne and bake the sweets directly on the oven shelf). Bake in a preheated oven at 180°C for 20-25 minutes, then turn out the sweets and leave them to cool on a rack.
In the meantime make the icing by beating the egg whites until they are not too stiff. Add the sugar and the lemon juice and continue to beat until the icing is dense and glossy. Carefully extract the minne from the moulds and spread the icing evenly on top. Once cold decorate the tip with a glacé cherry.

WATER ICES ARE THE MOST TYPICAL SUMMER BREAKFAST IN SICILY, PARTICULARLY IN THE PROVINCES OF MESSINA, CATANIA AND SIRACUSA. THEY ARE MOSTLY EATEN AT A BAR, DUNKING BRIOCHES SHAPED LIKE CHIGNONS INTO THEM, BUT IN SOME CASES THEY ARE STILL SERVED WITH SIMPLE DURUM WHEAT BREAD. PROFESSIONAL RECIPES REQUIRE THE USE OF GELLING AGENTS (FROM AGAR-AGAR TO CAROB SEED FLOUR BUT ALSO STARCH, ETC) WHICH GUARANTEE CREAMINESS AND MAKE THE ICE MORE RESISTANT TO MELTING. IN THIS CASE WE HAVE FAVOURED SIMPLE AND MORE TRADITIONAL RECIPES, WATER ICES WHICH WERE ONCE MADE AT HOME WITHOUT EVEN THE AID OF AN ICE-CREAM MACHINE. THE QUANTITIES OF SUGAR ARE MERELY INDICATIVE. WITH REGARD TO SWEETS AND, ABOVE ALL, COLD DESSERTS IT IS ENTIRELY A MATTER OF PERSONAL TASTE.

GRANITA DI MANDORLE (Almond water ice)

For 2 people

- 400 ml of almond milk
- 4-5 tablespoons of syrup sugar (cold)

Only use the syrup sugar if the almond milk is unsweetened. Mix the two ingredients and pour into an ice-cream machine. If you don't have one of these then pour the mixture into a low-walled container, preferably made of aluminium and place it in a freezer, scoring it with a fork every half hour so that it doesn't solidify into ice.

"If ever you didn't know, then know
now that down there the hot sun
extracts the fragrances from the trees.
Do not wonder at this: there lingers
in the air of that land a perfume
like a perfume of love".
Ibn Hamdis

Acknowledgments

This books owes many people a huge debt of gratitude. We would like to say a big thank you to Guido Tommasi, without whom this book would not have been written. It was while we were in conversation with him that the idea began to take shape, an idea which eventually turned into a challenge. His trust in us enabled us to see the project through. A heartfelt thank you goes to Alessandra who was with us from start to finish. Thank you Giusy, who found time to dedicate to the project in the midst of wedding preparations, thank you Laura for your painstaking and discreet hunt for typos and thank you Tommaso for your sensitive work on the colours and typeface.
Thank you Grandma Pina, who cooked for us and who spent hours on the telephone explaining recipes in detail over and over again. Thank you Aunt Graziella and Uncle Giovanni who welcomed us into their home and adapted it for our photo shoot. Thank you Uncle Maurizio for catching and cleaning about a hundred sea urchins and for finding the tastiest pink prawns we have ever eaten. Thank you Aunt Sara for cooking stewed cauliflower in not the most clement of seasons. Thank you Micaela, who was our quartermaster in the belly of Palermo and on the islands. Thank you Enza for your couscous and energy. Thank you Signora Angela for your bread and thank you Signore Sapienza for showing us your lush orchard and a garden of delights. Thank you Aldo for lending us a hand. Thank you Ilaria for helping with the cassata. Thank you Giacomo and Luca for being patient. Thank you Laura for your advice. Thank you Giacomo Alessi and Giovanni Alessi, who made our work more pleasant. Thank you Cris Vecli, who helped us find the right glass and the right teaspoon, thank you Spazio Sette store in Rome, and especially Rosanna and Gabriele for their courtesy and expertise. And thank you all those friends who shared their recipes with us sometimes waiting for hours until we had finished taking our photographs.

© Guido Tommasi Editore - Datanova S.r.l., 2015

Texts: Maria Teresa Di Marco, Marie Cécile Ferré
Photographs: Maurizio Maurizi
Translation: Judith Mundell
Graphics and page layout: Tommaso Bacciocchi

The ceramics photographed on pages 17, 27, 29, 47, 49, 51 and 53 are by Giacomo Alessi.

ISBN: 978 88 67531 110

Printed in China